Pond of

Scams

By

Tolu Ayoade

Tolu Ayoade
Visit my website at www.pondofscams.com

ISBN-13:
978-1532985805

ISBN-10:
1532985800

Table of Content

Preface

Acknowledgements

Introduction

Chapter 1 : The Fraud : Conventional and Internet

Chapter 2 : Deception

Chapter 3 : The Chaos and Reasons

Chapter 4 : Possible internet scam schemes and how to avoid them

Chapter 5 : Why do people fall into the scammers net?

Chapter 6 : Scam survival and reduction

Chapter 7 : Agencies to report internet scams to

Bibliography

Preface

We live in an age where we engage in online, real time financial transactions. Hundreds of millions of people shopping and engaging in one transaction or the other via web, mobile and POS, the common factor here is the payment mode which is internet based payment.

Many businesses transact via the web, individuals make purchases and sales through the web, the common denominator is the web, and hence there are so many scammers on prowl till they find an unsuspecting victim they can scam, through the deceptive moves they possess. Are you been scammed online, or are there some mails you have been replying that shouldn't be replying?

Some of the basic assumptions this book makes about you the reader is that you are a novice when it comes to being able to decipher a mail or scam, and taking preemptive move to curb.

Reading this book from cover to cover, takes you through a journey from understanding how the scammer takes to plotting scams, the possible internet scam schemes and how to curb such scams.

Acknowledgements

I will like to express my tremendous gratitude to the people I spoke to in the course of writing this book, those who have been a victim , those who had one time in their life perpetrated the credit card fraud or any of the internet scams and also those websites and blogs I used as reference for the scam letter samples.

This book stemmed out of the need to educate unsuspecting victims all over the world, guide them along a path that would ensure they do not fall a victim to the scammers on prowl out there in the larger fish pond.

Introduction

Scams have always been in existence since the 18th century and when the internet came it arrived with a lot of positivity, but later we saw conmen taking advantage of the invention, so they innovated and transformed their con strategy and plots which is being used to scam unsuspecting victims via the internet.

The entry level for internet scam now is so low that anyone that can use a computer could possibly learn how to scam and send out over 10,000 emails and wait for 10 people to respond to the emails and their plots will be initiated.

Many of the unsuspecting victims could have been easily scammed because they were not aware of the schemes deployed by the scammers, but some other people are scammed because they were greedy and they fell for the scammers, have you imagined what happens to a man that was sent a mail and he was told that his name was found in the will of a man from Texas he does not know and the scammers are asking him to send some money in order to process the inheritance fund, he sends processing , insurance and administrative fees only to discover he was scammed, the victim does not report the case to the authorities because he knows anyone who hears the story will not have pity on him because he was greedy, so he keeps it to himself and it is not added to the world statistics on internet scams.

The alarming rate at which unsuspecting victims fall for these scams shows that many victims are not equipped with the guide to help them recognize the scams when they are sent as emails, in order for the unsuspecting victims not to go through with the requests from the emails. This book is geared towards helping everyone stay alert and not fall for the internet scams.

Anyone can fall for an internet scam, the young to the old, from professors to lawyers, businessmen to financial experts, men and women, virtually everyone is liable to fall for internet scams. You need to have a guide to assist you in surfing the web, shopping, sending emails etc.

You will find this book very interesting and helpful, it is a book you need to buy for your dad, mum, siblings, uncles, aunties, friends, colleagues and even a boss that shops , transacts business online, books hotels and travels a lot. All those who have a very high level of vulnerability can easily be fell by the plot of the scammer, so you need this book to prepare for the whirlwind that lies ahead.

Reading this book will make you develop some paranoia whenever you want to reply emails from unknown sources or making payment with your card online, when you go through the many scam stories you will see in the chapter dedicated to possible internet scams.

Scam vulnerability quiz

I'm not naïve to think this is the first book you have read on internet fraud/scam, and I know you have read so many other books on internet fraud/scam so that you can be aware of the vices employed by the scammers. Some of you might have received scam letters and emails by scammers in the past, also some of you might have been scammed/duped. Take a few minutes to go through the quiz below and see if you can answer them with all sincerity.

As you go through the quiz below, put a mark where appropriate as it applies to you.

Check everything that applies and be a hard grader.

- Have you ever received a scam mail?
- Do you have a credit/debit card?
- Do you plan to shop online?
- Have you ever given out your credit/debit card details online?
- Do you always visit e-commerce websites, even if you have never bought anything?
- Do you get emails from companies advertising their products that can be purchased online?
- In a month do you get between 4 and 10 scam mails?
- You have changed your email address (free mail service) several times due to scam mails being sent to you.
- You have replied suspected scam mails in the past.
- You hold back personal information when you reply scam letters.

- You have once fallen victim by losing money to fraudsters.
- You have once changed your credit card because your credit card information was given out.

Chapter 1: The Fraud: Conventional and Internet

Internet fraud is basically the use of internet services to scam or defraud unsuspecting victims. Scammers had always scammed unsuspecting victims before the advent of the internet and this dates back to as far as over 120 years, sometime in the 18th century.

Advance fee scam started a long time ago as far back as the 18th century as I mentioned earlier, the conmen contacted their victims via posting mails and the victims were targeted and scammed, they needed to know the name or address of the victim they picked unlike what happens now where they can reach out through job boards, forums, social media and expect any unsuspecting victim to fall for their scam.

In some cases you could be wondering how they got your email address, the scammers scan through the web for email addresses using email extractors and then they have a large database to reach out to.

The Spanish prisoner scam started sometime around the 18th century, the scammer or fraudster tells the unsuspecting victim who is also referred to as his mark, that he has access to a high net worth individual who has been imprisoned in spain under a false identity.

The scammer tells the unsuspecting victims that he needs to raise money to secure the release of the imprisoned man before his identity is revealed, because his identity should never be revealed.

The victim is told that he/she should send money over for this cause, and when the prisoner is released the victim will be financially rewarded. The request for money will continue until the victim feels he/she has spent a lot and eventually declines further payment.

The advance fee fraud seemed to have had a smooth transition from pre-internet fraud age to internet age. Earlier before the advent of internet fraud you needed to know your victim's name before you address the letter to him/her or have the address or location, but right now the internet medium is so perfect for their scam, thereby making their scamming operation smooth, the fraudster still gets to be anonymous and thousands of emails are sent out to unsuspecting victims.

Chapter 2: Deception

Deception is an act of propagation of certain impressions of things that are not true to people, a misleading falsehood, and an act of deceiving unsuspecting victims.

There are several motives for deception to be carried out, either to protect the other person involved or to be self-focused about it. It is always very difficult to detect deception; you must have been trained in knowing how to detect deception.

Scammers have taken to deception in making their plots accepted by the unsuspecting victims, they believe every word of the scammer and even if a scammer requests for money three times during a scamming process they don't realize they have been duped until they lose so much money and decide to opt out. And so many people are too ashamed to report that they have been scammed because the deception was way too easy and only a greedy person could follow through with the plans of the scammer.

In some cases there is a camouflage or visual deception effect carried out on the victim, scammers backup claims of being a member of the US marines with pictures of a US marine taken off the internet, a box filled with gold gotten from the web or a room with a table stacked with bundles of dollar notes, all this is done in order to deceive their victim.

Their letters and plot are well thought out and played out sequentially, and in the case where they missed something out in their plot, they simply go back to the drawing board and remodel their deception.

Chapter 3: The Chaos and Reasons

The chaotic situation you are going through right now may have been caused by you and you have what it takes to get out of the situation, but what I can do for you is to give you a little push and you take the leap, which you would have to take without me but with this book in your hands.

I am not writing this book to dissuade you from clinching juicy contracts in Nigeria , Australia , Qatar or anywhere else in the world , am not also stopping you from going into business partnerships across the globe but to give you some steps and guidelines to follow.

Neither am I saying you should not participate in an internet auction nor an online lottery game.

1.   You are an extremely flexible person who thrives on new ideas but impetuous.

Flexibility should be exhibited by every individual and most especially business men because the more flexible an entrepreneur is the more open he/she is to new ideas and business/brand growth.

CEOs, entrepreneurs etc. know what am talking about, because they have been in running of businesses and they know what to do when an opportunity presents itself.

I have read of a CEO who exhibited high levels of flexibility in him, he took a company from a $4million dollar yearly profit to a $12 million dollar yearly dollar profit within a year due to his flexibility.

What do I mean by being flexible? It has to do with the openness to fresh ideas and opportunity, you creating a blue ocean before you due to other business factors around you that could have been staring you in the face or being planted by scammers.

Be flexible but cautious when taking on new ideas brought to you because some of the ideas could emanate from scammers trying to take advantage of your flexibility.

2.   You are under pressure because of the mails that you receive and some are reminders asking if you still want the deal or not.

This type of business or personal pressure can be attributed to the reason why some people were scammed, you receive an email from a scammer and the same email is sent repeatedly, after which the scammer follows up with reminders emphasizing how bad it will be for you to miss the offer or the urgency in the remittance of funds for the project being proposed.

I once received a mail from organizers of an IT conference a while back and I got interested, I replied the email and made some enquiries, within a few hours I got a response with the details requested, we went on at this for two weeks before I discovered they were scammers, this happened about six years ago and I had not sent money to them even though they requested. If you look deeply you will always see loopholes in their arrangements. Now when I get such mails I just delete them from my email box.

3.   You reply such mails rather than delete them.

Replying mails sent by scammers have listed you as a possible victim, so the moment they get your mail they mount pressure on you and see if you will break. I resulted to deleting suspicious emails I never reply them. You too should do same when you receive such.

4.   Who cares about my personal credit card information.

You think no one cares about your personal information? Oh, so many people do, because we have a lot of scammers out there ready to use that information that can make you lose so much money in dollars, pounds, naira, yen, francs etc.

The message will come in different mediums such as email, image advert via email, phone call, text messages, social media direct messages etc. Be very careful not to respond to these messages because they could lead to a downfall, don't click on links in emails.

We have so many scammers sending messages using different banks masked email addresses for individuals to click and update personal information which also includes their credit/debit card numbers and PINs, this is called phishing.

All they want to do is trick you into believing it is the bank that has sent these emails and hoping you would click on the link and enter the details requested. Banks have always stated in mails and SMS that they will never request for your personal bank details online or via phone calls. Don't click every link you see in your email.

5.   You see nothing wrong in wiring money.

You need to start seeing this as a problem, because if you are quick to wire transfer money to anyone on the internet, someday you could fall a victim for the scammers out there.

Be sure of the person requesting you to send money to them they could be scammers.

6.   You have no time reading your monthly statements.

You need to imbibe the culture of checking your bank statements periodically, this will help you notice some irregularities, what makes you so sure that some deductions have not been done on your cards, it may be as little is $1.30 , but imagine this happening every week on your account, you could be losing so much in a long run.

7.   All investments have their risks.

Do you get mails informing you of low-risk , high-return business investment opportunities , the pitches are just so good and smooth , they tell you it has a very low-risk so your money is safe and you will not lose money , and they say the business is a high-return one that ensures that you make almost 100% profit.

One thing you need to look out for is a business venture that sounds too good to be true, then it is probably too good to be true, hence, you need to be alert. They also come with so much urgency in the email asking you to act now else you lose out in the opportunity that has presented itself.

All businesses are meant to have risks, the people trying to scam you present this business as such that it has little or no financial risk, or demand that you send cash immediately to them to order the goods / machinery or register as a distributor. There are agencies they can be reported to, these agencies will be discussed later in the concluding chapters.

Fallacious

The mails or letters sent to the victims always sound too good to be true, why would you fall for a letter or mail that the writer says he is a bank manager in Nigeria and would like to transfer the $260 million to the receiver of the mail because a mark Jefferson died in Nigeria 20 years ago and left a huge fortune in Nigeria, and he had listed this mail receiver as a beneficiary when he died.

A question I would like to add is do you know any mark Jefferson who could include your name in a will? Do you have a relative or friend who goes by the name mark Jefferson? Can anyone list you as a next of kin without your knowledge?

The mail reads further as thus "since you are listed as the next of kin, I will like to contact you to furnish me with your bank details for immediate transfer of the funds to you, but if you don't have the required documents to collect this money, I could arrange them for you but it will cost you, I and the central bank governor will get to keep 30% of the $260 million while 60% is remitted into your account, the remaining 10% will be used to bribe some government officials in Nigeria so that the money transfer to you can be fast tracked. "

The receiver of the email is led to believe he can collect this money, he is sent documents with the government's logo authorizing him to receive the money from the apex bank in Nigeria. He is then told that they need to open an account in Nigeria which will be used to facilitate the transfer of the money to him, in the process of opening the account he is told to send 2% of the total money to be collected in order to open an account and process payment in Nigeria.

They know the victim is hooked so they inform him of the urgency in transferring 2% of the $260million to them, as the victim transfers this money, they come up with other requests for payments, the demand increases till the victim recognizes it is a scam.

Chapter 4: Possible internet scam schemes and how to avoid them

This chapter gives us an insight into the types of internet scams perpetrated by scammers and how you can know their various schemes, many people have fallen prey because they did not have an idea of the types of schemes available, and this book will help reduce the incidents recorded worldwide.

Internet Scam Schemes

Phishing scams

Advance Fee scams

Survey scams

Job scams

Over Payment scams

Lottery scams

Inheritance scams

Psychic & Clairvoyant scams

Hotel booking scams

Business Email Compromise scams

All these scams listed above will be treated in details and several examples of each given so as to keep us abreast with the latest scams being pulled by these scammers, we can help you identify the scams, but we have noticed that greed would still make many people fall for the pranks the scammers play.

Phishing Scam

They are typically fraudulent email messages perpetrated by attempting to acquire sensitive information such as usernames, passwords, and credit card details often for malicious reasons, by disguising as a trustworthy entity (your bank, university, email provider).

Most of the times these communications are claiming to come from banks, universities, internet service providers, online payment processors, popular social websites, auctions sites, email providers etc. to lure unsuspecting victims.

There are various methods being utilized to get the sensitive information from unsuspecting victims, emails or instant messages are sent and when a victim clicks on it, the victim is redirected to a fake website whose look and feel is identical to the legitimate one, the address bar might be masked and the URL seen is not what it is, this is done in order to make the victim believe it is the legitimate website.

Phishing has increased tremendously over the past few years, even though there has been consistent public awareness and legislation in place, but victims seem to be on the increase. Personally, I receive a minimum of 20 phishing campaigns weekly but all I do is delete them and in some cases I report to the legitimate website and firm, so that other not too lucky people will not be scammed if the website owner takes action to bring the website down.

Types of Phishing Scams

Spear phishing

This phishing type is directed at specific individuals or firms. The success rate of this attack is increased due to the extensive work done in gathering personal information on their target.

Whaling

This is basically spear phishing attacks directed specifically at senior executive officers or other high-profile targets within a business, government or organization.

The email content is crafted to appeal to the upper management and the senior executive officers; it makes them feel this mail is for their level of sophistication and professionalism.

How to avoid Phishing Scams

- You have to be suspicious of any organization or firm that requests for your confidential personal information (username, password, social security number, credit card number and PIN) in an email message, the moment you see such an email message then you have to delete without thinking for too long about the email.
- If you think the message could be legitimate then go directly to the company's website (type the URL into your browser to gain access to the company's website) or call the company to find out if they sent such an email and if

you really need to take such action as described in the email.

- Whenever you delete a suspicious phishing scam mail from your inbox, go to the deleted items folder and empty the folder. If you know you could easily fall for such emails then always read your mails in plain text so that all clickable images will show the URLS all the images point to, if you read emails in HTML your attacker could take advantage of your email client's ability to execute codes to run very simple scripts that makes your system vulnerable to further attacks or creates a pathway for the attacker for future access to your system or network.

- Be careful, banks will never contact customer by email to ask for passwords or any other sensitive information by clicking on a link.

- The phishing scam emails will in most cases have odd spellings in the subject box of the email and contain spelling and grammatical errors in the email. Most of the fraudsters don't know your name, so the email addresses you in vague terms eg. "Dear valued customer"

- Use your spam filter to filter such emails, if you detect a phishing email, mark the message as spam and delete it, this will ensure that in future the same message or messages from the same source does not get through to your email box.

- Some organizations have a team that is recruited and trained to monitor and take down any suspicious website or link that is used to phish their clients, this team is always recruited as permanent staffs or placed on a retainer scheme. Furthermore, never download attachments you are not sure of it's source, at times some attachments appear to be pdf files, but when you download such files you discover it is an EXE file which when clicked on, it installs itself on your system to phish for information in a stealth mode.

Examples of Phishing Scams

Sample 1

"From: "INDIANA.EDU SUPPORT TEAM" <supportteam01@indiana.edu>

Reply-To: "INDIANA.EDU SUPPORT TEAM" <supportteam@info.lt>

Date: Sat, 12 Jul 2008 17:42:05 -0400

To: <"Undisclosed- Recipient:;"@iocaine.uits.indiana.edu>

Subject: CONFIRM YOUR ACCOUNT

Dear INDIANA.EDU Webmail Subscriber

This mail is to inform all our {INDIANA.EDU} webmail users that we will be maintaining and upgrading our website in a couple of days from now. As a Subscriber you are required to send us your Email account details to enable us know if you are still making use of your mailbox. Be informed that we will be deleting all mail account that is not functioning to enable us create more space for new students and staffs of the school, You are to send your mail account details which are as follows:

*User Name:

*Password:

*Date of birth:

Failure to do this will immediately render your email address deactivated from our database.

Thank you for using INDIANA.EDU

FROM THE INDIANA.EDU SUPPORT TEAM "

Explanation

According to this email displayed above, which claims to be from the 'Support Department', they claim to be doing some maintenance and upgrading and you therefore need to provide them with some personal details to avoid problems or disruption of services.

However, the email is not from any legitimate service provider support department. It is a phishing scam designed to trick you into giving your email account login details to cybercriminals.

At this point, you may believe that you have resolved the supposed issue. However, the criminals can collect the information you submitted and use it to hijack your real email account. They can then use the account to send out spam and scam messages in your name.

Internet service providers may send out messages warning that your account is nearing or has exceeded its storage limit. However, such emails will clearly identify the service provider and they will not demand that you click a link to rectify the problem. It is always safest to login to your online accounts by entering the address into your browser's address bar or via an official app rather than by clicking a link in an unsolicited email.

Sample 2
"Dear Amazon.com Customer,

Amazon.com has recently updated our customer database and new security feature has been added to our website for effective shipping and order. Please click the link below to update your account information within 24-hours.

Click Here.

Thanks

Amazon.com"

Explanation

The email claims to be from amazon, saying due to the added security feature, the customer database had to be updated by the customer who needs to click on a link below to update their account information within 24-hours.

This email did not emanate from amazon, instead a scammer is using the popular phishing scam to steal the customers' personal and financial information.

When the click here link is clicked it takes the unsuspecting victim to a website well-crafted to look like the original amazon website, the customer will be asked to login with his/her amazon username/email address and password, further filling of the form requests for credit card details and the customer is redirected to the original amazon website.

Amazon will never send a mail to customers to click on a link to update personal/financial information, always type the URL into the address bar to enter online accounts.

Advance Fee scam

Advance fee fraud as the name implies is simply an email that is sent to someone, an individual or an investor, the person is asked to pay a fee up front or in advance of receiving any money, goods, services in order for the deal to sail through.

The victims are always told to pay a fee in exchange for money or goods to be sent to the unsuspecting victim, they could also be sought for assistance in movement of funds from a country in political turmoil.

The upfront fees paid are sometimes referred to as membership fees, participation fees, administrative fees, handling fees etc.

A lot of the advance fee fraud emails are also referred to as "419 fraud", 419 was derived from the article of the Nigerian criminal code that deals with fraud. The scam started in the 80s as mailed letters but has now evolved into emails.

Types of Advance Fee Scams

Beneficiary fund scam

The scammers send emails to their victims, these emails have some story about a large amount of money that is available in a bank in some other country that needs to me moved to the victim's country and the victims help is highly needed to make the movement of funds smooth and unhindered.

Urgency is emphasized in the mail, and the victim is told that if he/she does not act quickly the money will be confiscated by the government and once that is done the money can never be retrieved. In most cases the victims who fall for this type of scam are greedy, they want to reap where they did not sow, why would you be interested in getting paid for moving funds you know does not belong to you.

Inheritance scam

Inheritance scam occurs when a victim is contacted and told that someone very rich is dead and the dead person had the victim's name inserted in line to receive a huge inheritance.

The scammer presents himself as the lawyer who is in charge of administering the inheritance but was unable to locate the dead person's relatives, so he has found the victim because the victim shares the same surname with the dead person. He goes on to say if the victim doesn't collect the money early it will be confiscated by the government.

The victim is told never to tell anyone about the inheritance, urging the victim to deal in secrecy during the inheritance processing, the victim is asked to pay legal fees, administrative fees, taxes on the money about to be received. Once the money is received the victim will not hear from the scammers anymore, and it becomes clear that the person has been scammed.

Investment scam

Investment mails are sent to unsuspecting victims, requesting their assistance in investing money overseas through investment companies.

The victim is asked to pay some fees upfront in order for the investment opportunity to be presented to the victim. Furthermore, the victim is informed that the profit margin is high and this is the best opportunity the victim needs. As part of the investment processes the victim is asked to pay some money as processing fees, legal fees, administrative fees after which he victim can invest in the business or can be made a franchisor.

As soon as this money is paid that, the scammer will try to request for more money or just trash his phone lines and will be unreachable.

Loan scam

This scam is not only aimed at those trying to get loans, in some instances they know many people have at least one loan hanging on their neck which they are trying to get out of, So when the victim receives an email from the scammers, it is because they sent out over 10,000 emails and they believe some of the emails will go out to people who had at some point taken loans from banks or other financial institutions, they are told they can help them in the loan repayment. They send forms for the victim to fill after which the victim is asked to send some money for the loan application to be processed.

After a while the victim gets a mail that the loan has been approved, they ask for additional information and supporting documents, after which the victim receives another email requesting for some fees (insurance, administrative) and in some instances they request for about two to three months advance payment after which they promise to send the check to the victim. Which the victim never receives.

Other formats the scammers employ are mails emanating from the scammer claiming to step in to stop a foreclosure or get loans modified, they could also ask the unsuspecting victim to pay them the money instead of the mortgage company because they claim to be interested in helping the victims transfer the funds to the mortgage company and seek for lower fees in future and to reduce the number of months left for the payment.

Romance and Dating scam

Victims are seen as lonely people who need some companion and they find this companion or friends through the internet chat rooms or social media sites, they become friendly with the victim and then start sending mails requesting assistance.

They could be asking for money to assist sick and bed ridden relatives, or asking for money to replace stolen items like phone and other personal belongings. In some cases they request for finances that will make them secure visas and air fare to meet their lover (the victim).

It is always a well-orchestrated plot, from how the scammer meets the unsuspecting victim, to building trust, then putting forward a story that would make the victim have some pity on him, after this trust has been bought and the scammer knows the victim will show empathy, the scammer starts requesting for monetary assistance.

We have had instances where a lady in Europe falls in love with a man in a chat room, social media site, forum site etc. The new lover sends fake pictures to the unsuspecting victim, giving the impression that the picture sent belongs to the lover, the scammer will always prefer to make phone calls through the conventional phones, every time the unsuspecting lover(the mark) suggests they skpe or use other forms of internet messaging service that uses video, the scammer will always have an excuse, because he does not want to be seen.

Work from home scam

This kind of scam is always a get-rich-quick scam where the unsuspecting victim looks for a job online and is lured by a mouthwatering offers of employment at home, The income is always too huge to be true, and the amount of effort put in is little. The attraction is the fee the scammer is telling the victim to pay to join the scheme or to get the job with the company.

Some would tell the victim they need a professional that can do database migration, edit a script, proof read a book etc. When the victim says he/she has got no database design / administration skills, editing skills the scammer would propose to train and offer certificate for as little as $200, and wait for the victim to fall for the scam.

The scammer could collect the training fees, and request for membership fees, by the time the unsuspecting victim wakes up from the scamming sleep, he/she would have lost a minimum of $300, now imagine someone losing $300 to three different scammers in four months, that is $900 lost, this is money that could have been saved or invested.

Online sales and rentals scam

The scammers send a fake check to the seller of an item on ebay or any of the websites, sellers place items / products for sale. The scammer's check will have an amount greater than the cost of the item online, the scammer tells the seller to kindly send the difference to him via wire transfer.

The seller will be happy a sale has been made and in the midst of the eagerness the seller sends the difference to the scammer via wire transfer, by the time the check clears he will discover the check was declared fake in the bank and he had been scammed.

Another scenario plays out when it is the scammer that places the item on the site (craiglist , ebay etc) to sell, the scammer does not have the intention of exchanging any item for money, the plan is to place a high-priced consumer electronics like laptops, expensive phones, high end cameras and expensive wristwatches on the internet for sale at a price far below the retail price in stores or online malls, for example a professional video camera that costs $6,000 is placed for sale at $2,100 , this offer will get any web visitor who knows about cameras to be interested in acquiring such a camera. Then they extract money from the buyer in guise of buying additional accessories or probably ask the buyer to wire transfer the money and promise that the gadget will be shipped in 3 to 4 business days, after they receive the money they would most likely discontinue the use of the phone line and buy another sim card.

Pet scam

This type of scam is carried out by the scammer putting up an advert for the sale of a pet on any of the websites that allows sellers to sell their items like ebay , craiglist etc.

The moment someone shows interest in the pet they send a mail to the buyer with a few questions to elicit some personal information from the pet buyer who is about to be scammed. The information elicited will be name, income status and location of the buyer.

The location of the buyer is very necessary for the scammer, because the scammer's next email is meant to be an excuse email why the buyer might not be able to see the pet before payment is made, all the buyer gets to see is the picture of the pet via the internet, because the buyer has told the scammer his/her location, the scammer regrets his unavailability because he/she is far away from the buyer, this is because he/she knows the location of the buy, so the information is used against the buyer.

In an event where the buyer claims he/she can come over the location of the pet, the scammer sends another mail on how something came up and will have to leave town for a few days, all these is done so that they will never meet in person with the buyer, hence, the buyer never gets to see the pet and pay for the pet, because there is no pet to be sold. They keep postponing because they want the unsuspecting victim to get fed up of excuses and then send the money over.

Many people have been scammed using this pet scam, because of their love for pets, they were hoping to buy a pet or adopt one where necessary.

You must insist that you need to see the pet you are about to pay for, before payment is made.

How to avoid Advance Fee Scam

To avoid this type of scam check out the following below:

- Use common sense to interpret the emails.
- If it sounds too good to be true, then it probably is.
- Never send money to anyone you don't know through wire transfer.
- Upfront fees payment should deter you from any transaction.
- Pressure to act immediately by a sender of mail you do not know should be an indicator for fraud.
- Request for personal information must never be granted by you.
- Distance yourself from anyone who sends you a mail guaranteeing you a loan if you pay in advance.
- Avoiding filling out forms in email messages asking for personal information.
- Delete suspicious emails from your mailbox.
- An indication is when the request contains a sense of urgency.
- The sender repeatedly requests confidentiality.
- Guide your account information carefully.
- Do not believe the promise of large sums of money for your cooperation.

Examples of Advance Fee Scams

Sample 1
"Deaerst,

How are you today?

It is my pleasure to contact you for a business venture which I and my junior sister (Sandra) intend to establish in your country.

Though I have not met with you before but I believe, one has to risk confiding in succeed sometimes in life. There is this huge amount of eight million U.S dollars($8,000,000.00) which my late Father kept for us with a Fiduciary Fund Holder in Abidjan before his sudden death during this war in Cote d'ivoire.

Now I and my sister have decided to invest these money in your country or anywhere safe enough outside Africa for security and political reasons. We want you to help us claim and retrieve these fund from the Fiduciary Fund Holders and transfer it into your personal account in your country for investment purposes on these areas:

1). Telecommunication 2). The Transport Industry 3).Car trading If you can be of an assistance to us we will be pleased to offer to you 15% Of the total fund.

You can call me on this line for more detail: +00000000000 [real number]

I await your soonest response.

Respectfully yours,

Miss. Ceilline Milan"

Explanation

First and foremost let's look at the spelling of dearest, the first word we see in the mail, they don't get some spellings right at times, and same message goes to different people all over the world. Dearest is spelt as " Deaerst " , this could get you prepped for what is about to come.

The victim is promised 15% of the total fund, the offer should alert the victim that this is a fraudulent person sending the mail. The sender of the mail picked your email address , you never told him/her you were interested in wealth management for a client.

Sample 2

"Email Subject: Awaitting your responce.

My name is Danjuma Sule, one of the sons of major Gen Gumel Danjuma Sule, The late Nigeria's former minister of mines and power in the regime of the late former Nigeria's military Head of state, Gen Sanni Abacha.

He married my mother on the agreement that my mother,Amina Fausat Sule, will maintain her family's name together with her children. Before he died in the German hospital on the 15th of November 1988 where he went to operate on the cancer of the knee, he fixed the Sum of $30,000.000.00 in the Central Bank of Nigeria under Intartrade Ventures Ltd on behalf of my mother. The 3 yrs maturity period placed on the money is due but the problem we are having now is that we lost the whole of the documents as a result of fire, which gutted our house 3 months ago.

We have discussed with our family attorney on how to collect the money with out hitches, he advised us to liaise with a foreigner who will act as the foreign partner of Intartrade Ventures Ltd and will purport that The money in question is urgently needed overseas for an important project.

It is on this basis I am seeking for assistance. Your percentage is negotiable. Please note; your age and profession doesn't really matter in this transaction. Waiting for your immediate response.

Regards,

Danjuma Sule"

Explanation

The first line shows a wrong spelling of the word awaiting , some other words are wrongly spelt as is typical of scam emails.

The mail explains to the victim before commitment that he is being brought in illegally to claim a partnership that never existed, It is clear only a greedy person would fall for this type of fraud, the total sum of money is tempting, a whopping sum of $30 million , anybody that replies such email to show interests will be swindled.

The victim is made to part with some money that will be sent to the scammer in Nigeria, they probably say the money will be used to bribe some officials of the bank and also some ore to be paid as administrative fee in the bank.

"My Dearest,

How are you today hope all is well and fine? mine is a little bit hot over here in Dakar Senegal. Please i wish to tell you all about my self now. Because i am taking you as my everything please try to be there for me. I have choose you with my whole heart no matter that we have not seen each other in person before. But i believe that this is how God want it.

Meanwhile, I'm from ivory-coast, but due to the war in my country, that cost the dead of my father and my mother which made me to stay here as a refugee in Dakar Senegal. my condition here is terrible, Its just like one staying in the prison and i hope by Gods grace i will come out here soon. with your help I don't have any relatives now whom i can go to all our relatives ran away in the middle of the war the only person i have now is

Rev. Paul David. who is the pastor of the (Christ the king Churches) here in the camp. He has been very nice to me just like a father, since i came here. The Pastors Tel number is (00221-77-39-32-714) and his Name is Rev. Paul David.

Please if you call tell him that you want to speak with me he will send for me in the hostel, I'm leaving in the women's hostel (in the camp) because here they have two hostels one for the men the other for women.

My choosing you is a question i knew you must ask and i think it is a good question. i have two reasons for choosing you, i chooses you because it is the will of God. And i believe knowing you will bring hope back again to my life. My choosing you does not mean i do not have anybody to choose or trust. I have two uncles, that is my late fathers junior brothers whom i think are suppose to be taking care of me but they are also dead now. So i am left alone.i get your contact in Facebook.com

Please listen to this, i have my late father's Deposit Certificate of account and death certificate (as his next of kin) here with me which i will send to you latter, because when he was alive he deposited some amount of money in a leading bank in United kingdom which he used my name as the next of kin. The amount in question is $6.5m(Six Million Five Hundred Thousand Dollars).

I would like you to help me transfer this money to your account and you assist me to invest the money In your country and also to make arrangement on how i will come over and stay with you and continue my life and education. in your country immediately after the transfer is been done. I can not take the money myself because of my orphanage status in this country. I want you to send me your contact information below here so that I will send it to the bank immediately and also use it and introduce you to the bank as my foreign partner for the transfer. Your Name; .... Country; .... Address; .... Age; .... Telephone; .... Sex;..... Occupation; ....

I have contacted the bank and made them to know of my intention to withdraw this money, I also got them aware of the death of my late father and they have checked with all its take's and confirmation. However, the bank advice me that I should get in touch with a very responsible/trusted person who will stand on my behalf as my foreign partner in relation to withdraw the money. since I am currently in orphanage status here and would not be allowed to handle that amount of money. So I urgently need your humble assistance to move this money to your bank account that is why I felt happy when I saw your contact because I strongly believe that by the grace of God, you will help me invest this money wisely.

I am ready to pay 20% of the total amount to you if you can help me in this transaction and another 10% interest of annual after Income to you, for handling this transaction for us, which you will strongly have absolute control over.

Because of my condition here i don't have any right or privileged to some things be it money or whatever, because it is against the law of this country. as you know am a refugee here in Senegal i only use the computer in the office of our reverend father's office every morning when i am cleaning his office because am the one cleaning his office, so after my work i used his computer to check/write my mail, I want to go back to my studies because i only attended my first year before the tragic incident that lead to my being in this situation now took place.

Please, note that this transaction is 100% risk free and I hope to start the transaction as quick as possible.

I will like you to send me your pictures thanks and also try to call me as i requested so that we can hear each other's voices, my favorite language is English but our official language is French, but i speak English very fluently because i attended an American and English speaking private school in my country. i have a lot to tell you, i will be thinking about you so much, as i will be waiting to hear from you soonest. Please and please try to keep every thing about me to your self alone ok. have a wonderful day my dear.

Yours sincerely,

Miss Clara Mikando"

Explanation

Firstly, did you notice the grammatical errors, they were numerous and anyone could easily see that the person/people that crafted this mail are not well grounded in English language. The scammer try's to catch a fish (victim) into his/her net.

The victim is promised 30% of the huge sum of $6.5 million dollars which he did not work for, just by providing some details and awaiting the transfer to his account. The victim will assume a bored lady came across his facebook profile online and instantly fell in love, this scheme is just the beginning of a much bigger scheme to scam the unsuspecting victim who thinks this is a dating process, later he will discover it is a dating scam.

Survey Scam

This form of scam can be very tricky because those individuals who are not greedy could still fall for this type of scam; reason why they fall easily is because the unsuspecting victim thinks he/she is responding to a company's market research which will be used for statistical analysis.

Market research companies have been very instrumental in helping businesses gather feedback from users and customers, this feedback is used for forecasting, mostly, based on the request of the sales and marketing department.

The people who had been scammed in the past using the survey scam actually thought they were helping a company fill online survey forms to help with a marketing research project, so they freely give out some personal information, in other cases financial reward is promised if the survey is filled.

Types of Survey Scams

Online survey scam

We have so many easy-money schemes out there and online surveys are one of them, there are promises that if you complete questionnaires online you will get paid and this affects your judgment, you are thinking of the money you could receive and you fill a form to register and personal information is entered.

Many people have become victims because everyone wants to win money and since it is just a form that is meant to be filled, then they just start filling. People have access to laptops, computers, tablets and mobile phones, so it makes it easy for them to fill the forms and enter their personal information, people fall for this scam in their thousands because you are not sending money so you believe is not a scam, but it is, because your personal information is being taken from you and used against you, one of the ways it could be used against you is identity theft, also your details will go into their database as a spamming list and you will get bombarded by offers later.

Offline survey scam

Some scammers are out there using questionnaire forms to collect personal information from unsuspecting people by approaching you as a field data collector gathering data for a market research or census.

How to avoid Survey Scams

- Never pay anyone to take a survey.
- Any marketing research company will provide company information which you can verify, their address must be known, and they must have a website that will contain all the information under about us page.
- Find out if the company is legit before embarking on the survey.
- If a popular company is taking a survey the post should come from their email address, facebook fanpage , or URL.

Examples of Survey Scams

Sample 1

" Jetstar '11th Birthday First Class Flights Giveaway' Facebook Scam

This Facebook post, which comes from a Page that claims to be associated with Australian airline, Jetstar, is supposedly offering the chance to win first class flights plus $10,000 spending money. The Page claims that the giveaway is a way of celebrating the airline's 11'th birthday. The post features an image of a gift box containing a Jetstar airline ticket. To win, claims the message, all you need do is like and share an image, comment 'Happy Birthday' and click a link to claim your prize.

But, in fact, the Page is not associated with Jetstar in any way and it is certainly not giving away free airline tickets or cash. The Page is a typical Facebook scam designed to trick you into supplying your personal information on suspect prize pages.

If you like, share, and comment as instructed, you effectively become a spammer for the people who created the fake Page. Liking, sharing and commenting ensures that the scam travels rapidly around Facebook and is seen by a great many potential victims.

Clicking the link takes you to a third-party website that asks you to supply your name and contact details for a chance to win airline tickets. But, fine print on the site informs you that the information you supply will be shared with the site's 'sponsors'. Thus, after providing your details, you will begin receiving phone calls, emails, text messages, and surface letters advertising a host of products and services that you probably don't want or need.

The real Jetstar Facebook Page is simply called 'Jetstar Australia' and the official name of the company is 'Jetstar Airways', not 'Jetstar Airline'. The scammers have named their fake page in a way that may convince many people that the Page really is associated with Jetstar.

In recent months, like-farming and survey scammers have created fake Facebook Pages that falsely claim to be associated with several major airlines, including, Delta, Qantas, and Virgin. Be wary of any Facebook Page or post that claims that you can win free air travel or other valuable prizes such as cruises or luxury cars just by liking and sharing and participating in surveys or offers."

Explanation

Most people who see this post will definitely think it has emanated from jetstar airways , so they are quick to like the post , or share the contents of the post with their friends on facebook, furthermore, a link is provided on the post , when you click on the post it takes you to a website with a form requesting you to enter your personal information.

Many companies who send spam messages for several companies advertising their products and services utilize this scheme to gather personal information and also take advantage of the facebook shares you initiate to reach out to your facebook friends.

Sample 2

"Kroger '40% off voucher' survey

Complete these steps below to get your kroger 40% off!

1. Step 1, share

2. Post comment to facebook: " Thanks!" to get your 40% off

3. Final step: Click Like!"

Explanation

This post is distributed on facebook, and it is fraudulent because if you participate you will not win any voucher. The moment you share the post you have introduced the scam to all the people connected to you on facebook, and when a person clicks on the post the person is taken to the fake page that is setup by the scammer.

What we need to understand is that liking, sharing and commenting on the post will most definitely get all facebook friends exposed to the scam and some of them will follow the instructions of the first victim on that path and like, share and comment.

The scam could take the different victims to other websites or pop up web pages and request for personal information to be filled, the people who setup this fake facebook post might need to gather personal information for some companies that have offered to pay them commissions.

Job Scam

These are job offers that are presented to unsuspecting victims with exceptionally high and mouthwatering salaries and benefits, the salaries will always urge you to want to leave your present job and get into this new fictitious company.

Some schemes had published job openings in local newspapers or sent emails with job offers to their victims listing available job offers and promising to get them work visas and air fare out of the country for resumption but requesting the victim has to pay his hotel accommodation for two days pending the final interview and placement in a department in the firm.

Many people become victims because when they get such a mail they are not so sure they did not apply for the job, because as job applicants you must have applied for so many jobs via the internet or postage.

The job offers look so tempting and even at times they send out job openings meant for a supervisory role but tell you there is no job experience needed, could this be true, remember if it sounds too good to be true, then it probably is.

Types of Job Scams

Entry-Level job scam

Many job scams are carried out for entry-level positions, this happens mostly in the oil and gas sector, ports, warehousing, entertainment sector and IT sector. A recruiter posts job openings on job boards and forums about entry-level positions in the oil and gas sector with little or no experience and skills.

The entertainment industry is also witnessing this scam for entry-level positions, a call could be made on a forum for production assistants on movie sets, it does not require any experience or skills, so many people would apply and a plot is initiated to scam them of the little money they have on them, the recruiter might say he needs them to wire transfer just $200 for him to initiate their job processing and send it to the movie producer for approval, once the victim pays, he/she will never be contacted again, the scammer would move on to other unsuspecting victims.

Work at home job scam

The initiators of this type of scam are aware that many people want to stay at home and do multiple jobs via the computer and internet, and still get paid through wire transfers.

This type of fraud had been existing for a long time and they know people will always fall for their pranks.

Some work at home schemes have been known to request for personal information to process the applicants job application, this is all they need, they do not need to ask you for money.

Jobs on legitimate job boards scam

Some boards or forums have been known to be run by people with impeccable character, those we can refer to as been trustworthy.

Despite the fact that the board is legitimate, the scammers who place job ads on it have an intention to defraud anyone that visits the board.

Email from recruiter or employer job scam

The recruiter or the employer starts by telling you how capable you are for the job and how perfect you are as a candidate for the new job opening.

The next mail you will receive from them is a request for your personal information that will be used to complete your application.

How to avoid Job Scams

- Never pay any company or recruiter that says you need to pay before they get you a job, no excuse should be made for the money being requested from you.
- Be wary of emails with spelling mistakes and grammatical errors, those errors will give you an idea they are from some people sitting in a house without proper education to spot such mistakes , but looking for who to scam.
- Be careful and thread softly when you receive job offers from companies you never applied to.
- Always do an extensive research on a company that has offered you a job, most companies have websites, so that's a good place to start your findings or find out their company address and location and if possible visit the company if they do not have a website.
- Do you know if you do a google search on a company you could see some links to peoples comments about them or know if they have been blacklisted or talked about for scamming job applicants.
- When you are given an offer without an interview then you need to be careful, maybe you are being scammed, some even do an interview via a social media platform and not ask questions about the job description or position you are meant to fill.

Examples of Job Scams

Sample 1
"Dear XXXX XXXXX,

Our firm is known as a payment processor with services designed for international small companies.

Our firm have tracked your resume from CareerBuilder database reviewed it and think that you to be a perfect applicant for this job which we have.

Our Organization are now looking for a few qualified individuals for a vacant position "Check Assist Manager".

The main activity of this job is to collect payments [ACH transfers and checks] from our clients in United States.

Every check will be accompanied with detailed brief.

If you don't have checking account our manager will help you to open a new account.

Average income is $600-$800 per week.

Basic Requirements:

- *Honesty, responsibility and promptness in operations*

- *Computer skills [MS Word] personal e-mail address*

- *not less than 21 years old*

- *Available 6-10 hour per week;*

- *Ability to work at home*

- *US Citizenship*

It is a part-time job which doesn't require leaving your main job

NO START-UP FEE

Interested candidates please visit our web-site"

Explanation

The mail was sent from a free email address, a company that can request for someone with such job description should have a corporate email address. The sender of the email address make the job offer very interesting and the basic requirements are such that anyone can easily meet.

So many people will meet the requirements and it means more people to scam when they eventually show their interests, later on monies could be requested from the job applicants.

Sample 2
"QANTAS AIRWAYS

http://www.qantas.com.au/

Email: qantasoffice@globomail.com

Job Reference: Qts 012/014NSW

Dear Sir/Madam,

Qantas Airline is a diverse international carrier with over 10,000 foreign employees worldwide. Qantas Airline take pride in being the face of Qantas in many different countries, all over the world. Our Local and international crew operates over 900 flights each week, often on the new A380 aircraft. Our Flight Attendants are natural, genuine and engaging people who compliment our world-class premium brand.

Representing Qantas brings great opportunity for everyone who joins this dynamic team environment. Meeting new people is a daily occurrence and travelling to unique international destinations presents an exciting new way of life.

VACANCIES: UNLIMITED FOR THOSE IN THE (AVIATION INDUSTRY, IT,

PROJECT MGT. ADMINISTRATION, HOSPITALITY, MANAGERIAL OPENINGS)

1: Aero Engine Jobs
2: Aerodynamics/Fluids Jobs
3: Air Traffic Control Jobs
4: Aircraft Interiors Jobs
5: Airline/Office Jobs
6: Accounting Jobs
7: Administration Jobs
8: Cabin Crew Jobs
9: Cargo jobs
10: Chefs Jobs
11: Customer Relations/Pass. Service Jobs
12: Design Jobs
13: Sales & Marketing
14: Executive Cabin Crew Jobs
15: Finance Jobs
16: Fitters Jobs
17: Flight Simulation Jobs
18: Freight Jobs
19: Front Office Jobs

20: Grad. + Apprentice Jobs
21: Host & Hostess Jobs
22: I.T. Jobs
23: Landing Gear Jobs
24: Licensed Maint (Base) Jobs
25: Licensed Maint. (Line) Jobs
26: Marketing Jobs
27: Pilots Jobs
28: Mechanical, Technical & Electrical Jobs
29: Quality / Safety Jobs
30: Operations Jobs
31: Paint sprayers Jobs
32: Retail Jobs
33: Sales and Purchasing Jobs
34: Ground Staff
35: Systems/Softer/Comms Jobs
36: Stewards
37: Ticketing & Reservation Officer
38: Flight Stewards
39: Customer Service Agent

Contract duration 5 years (renewable prospects of securing permanent positions)

Contract/ job location: Australia

Do you have what it takes to deliver an exceptional customer experience?

NOTE: Candidates will be accessed according to their respective area of specialization.

Interested Candidates should immediately send their UPDATED resume to: qantasoffice@globomail.com <mailto:qantasoffice@globomail.com>

Yours Faithfully

Qantas Airways

Recruitment department

qantasoffice@globomail.com <mailto:qantasoffice@globomail.com>

Skype: hrdqantas"

Explanation

The email never emanated from Qantas Airways, but a scammer waiting for the unsuspecting victim to show interest by sending a resume to the email address provided, as soon as the reply is sent, the scammer goes into the next plot to request for money from the victim.

The unsuspecting victim is told to pay upfront fees to cover various expenses, the money is sent and after a few months of back and forth the victim stops receiving emails from the scammer and their job is done.

OverPayment Scam

The procedure for this is very easy, a seller puts up an item on ebay or any other online sales website for sale, a scammer sends the seller check or money order for an item he/she wants to buy from the seller, the amount on the fake check is always more than the amount the item was supposed to be sold for.

The scammer tells the seller to kindly wire the difference back to him that it was a mistake or the scammer could also say the difference is meant to buy some accessories which will be used with the gadget, he also goes ahead to provide the details of who the accessories seller is and how urgent it was for the victim to send the difference within a few hours. All this is done before the check clears, but you and I know the check will never clear because it's a fake check.

How to avoid OverPayment Scams

- Whenever a buyer sends you an amount more than the price of your item, send back the check and ask for the actual amount but if the distance is very far, take the check to your bank and wait for the check to clear and after you have received value, you can send back the difference, but I assure you anyone that overpays you is trying to scam you, that means the check will never clear.
- You need to know the full details of your buyer, their full name, address and phone number.
- Never agree to repay the difference until the check as cleared.
- Never send the item to the buyer until the check has cleared.
- Resist any pressure to start now.
- At times it is dangerous to pay the check into your bank, because it could be a forged check that could be under scrutiny later, investigations could prove the check was stolen and forged.
- It could also be a way to launder money by the scammer, remember the trail leads to you, because the check passed through your account.

- Always check for some warning signals in the emails sent by the scammers, the signals are wrong spellings, poor grammar, and excessive emphasis and capitalization.
- When the buyer insists on wire transfer, don't wire transfer.

Examples of OverPayment Scams

Sample 1

"I am Frederick N Dawson a representative of a modeling company situated in Bristol, United Kingdom. Your picture hads been selected for a billboard advertment/and local advert here at heathrow airport.Your pictures had been accepted by the Agency Ghost Inc

You will receive a check payment for the contract.You will deduct 15% of the check payment for using your gorgeous pictures for billboard advert; and proceed to sending the balance over to your appointed Agent via western union Money Tranfer for Legal Documentation of the deal and "Comp card".This payment will also be used as "Sign up fee" with the agent

We awaiting to receive four picture of you.The photos required is basically for a Coca cola advertment bill board at Heathrow airport in london..Let us know your decision ASAP."

Explanation

This mail when received will make the receiver very happy to be sent a mail requesting for his picture to be used in an advertisement. The moment the unsuspecting victim accepts the request and sends his/her photographs over, another mail is received requesting for an account number to send his/her payment to.

A check could be sent or money transferred into the account number provided, the amount on the check will always be more than the amount agreed, for example if $3,000 is agreed up, the scammer will send a check of $5,000, but when the receiver contacts the sender that the money was over paid, he/she is asked to send the balance to an account number provided, later on the victim discovers that the check never cleared because it was a fake check.

In the case where money is transferred, the money over paid will be asked to be paid into another account number, then later on the account owner could be visited by Interpol because the scammer could have hacked someone's account and transferred the money to the victim so the victim cashes the money and sends to the scammer, all traces to the scammer is destroyed but there is a trail to the victim.

Sample 2
"Thanks for your mail, I am really interested in the (plymouth),Fine i will pay $200 for it,Please i will want to indicate my mode of payment to you since i am not in the United States at the moment and there is a Company in the United States that is indebted to me in the amount of $3,500,So i will want to really seek your Assistance at this point, That i will want you to forward to me the the following informations below

that i will need to forward to the Company indebted to me so that they can make out the payment directly to you and after you have cashed it in your bank,You will have the excess amount on the payment sent to my International Shipping agent via WESTERN UNION MONEY TRANSFER ,All charges you are to pay at the western union office when sending the excess amount of $3,300 should be deducted from my balance,So you don't have to bother yourself about that, The reason for this is that,The Company indebted to me say they cannot make out the payment in two installment except once, And since i am purchasing your (plymouth) from you at this time,I will want to really be sure that my funds will be safe in your hands as i will want to entrust my money unto your care,So inorder for us to complete the purchase of the (plymouth) now,I will want you to get back to me with the following informations inorder for me to forward it to the Company indebted to me inorder for them to make out the payment in your name and send it to you ithout any furtherdelay, The following informations that i will require from you are as follows,

1] YOUR FULL NAME TO BE WRITTEN ON THE CHECK,

2] YOUR DIRECT HOUSE ADDRESS WHERE YOU WILL WANT THE PAYMENT TO BE SENT TO,

3] YOUR DIRECT CELL PHONE NUMBER THAT YOU CAN BE REACHED AT ANYTIME OF THE DAY SO THAT I CAN GIVE YOU A CALL SO THAT I CAN EXPLAIN TO YOU BETTER,

Upon receipt of this informations i have just requested from you,I will immediately forward it to the Company indebted to me to make out the payment in your name and send it to you immediately,I will be awaiting your response as soon as you get this mail,Do confirm this mail and get back to me as soon as possible.

Thanks "

Explanation

As we can see from the mail above, a seller that had [laced an item on sales gets the mail above from the buyer, the buyer is accepting to buy the item for $200, but the mode of payment is suspicious, he starts by saying he is not in the United States and he has a company that is indebted to him to the tune of $3,500.

He suggests that the company indebted to him in the United States, sends the seller a check of $3,500 while he deducts his $200 and sends the balance of payment to the buyer via western union money transfer, the balance will be $3,300. He goes ahead to ask for some personal information, This will enable the scammer have the address to send the check to.

If you need to avoid such scam, never send money to anyone via western union money transfer, and also wait for the check to clear before paying any outstanding to anyone on the internet.

Lottery Scam

This could be referred to as a type of advance fee fraud, fraudsters contact unsuspecting victims informing them of their lottery wining which is always a large amount in an overseas or online lottery. Once you respond to that email they request for your personal information, passport photograph and proof of identity for them to clarify and start processing your payment.

Once you reply with the information requested they see that you are on board and have seen you as a possible victim, so they start asking you to send various fees for the payment process to be complete and have your winnings transferred to you.

They ask for legal fees so that their legal department can finish legal processing and move it to the account department, once you pay you get another mail saying you need to pay taxes on the money won and administrative fees, they also request for your bank details where the money will be transferred to.

As soon as they get the fees you have sent in, you will not hear from them again. Most of this lottery scams are predominately Canadian, Australian and Spanish.

How to avoid Lottery Scams

- No legitimate lottery requests advance fees when you win.
- If you did not purchase a lottery ticket or enter for a lottery, there is no way you can win because you never entered for it.
- Disregard any communication from a lottery company, if you did not enter for it.
- Lookout for wrong spellings and grammatical errors, those are indications that the lottery is scam.
- You are told to keep your winnings confidential for security reasons.

- Never give your credit card information or bank details to anyone saying you won a lottery you did not buy a ticket for.
- Be wary of demands to send additional money to be eligible for future winnings.

Examples of Lottery Scams

Sample 1

"THE PRIZE AWARD DEPARTMENT CONTINENTAL LOTTERIES S.A.

C/O´DONNELL 306,

28830 MADRID

SPAIN.

Ref: CL/ES/1026-9172

Batch: 31-2404/05

22-02-2005.

WINNING NOTIFICATION.

Congratulations first category prize winner! You have been selected as one of six winners of the Worldwide Continental Lotteries, Madrid-Spain, online ballot, drawn for January 2005, therefore will be a privileged receiver of the grand prize of €531,220.17 (FIVE HUNDRED AND THIRTY ONE THOUSAND,TWO HUNDRED AND TWENTY EUROS,

SEVEVTEEN CENTS ONLY).Your e-mail address was attached to the winning number 5-11-14-20-31-45. Draw serial: 055. This lottery is promoted and sponsored by multinationals companies of the european union. We in the Worldwide Continental Lotteries, Spain is by this program, diversifying our online balloting lotteries draws, developed and designed to satisfy the cravings of the ever growing number of participants in our various programs. With funds accrued from previous draws and unclaimed prizes, payouts to all winners is guaranteed and payments in a record time. After randomly selecting 25,000 participants from an initial database of 4.500.000 emails and zonings, by their respective continents from across the World, we produced an extensive list from which you have emerged as one of the lucky winners of the Grand Draw prize.

To process your winnings and prize payment, you are to get in contact with;

Mr. JORGE DIAZ (Prize claims handler)

e-mail: diazge@yahoo.es

Tel: +34 62 8091594

You are advised to keep your winning informations confidential untill your claim is processed and your money remitted to you in whatever manner you prefer. This is in line with our security policies, to avoid double claims and misapropriations of the Lottery funds as it has happened in the past. Direct all further communications and enquiries to your category prize claim handler and remember to include your reference and batch numbers. Congratulations once again from Continental Lotteries. Thank you for being part of our promotional program.

Sincerely,

JAVIER OCHOA SUAREZ

INTERNATIONAL ONLINE COORDINATOR

CONTINENTAL LOTTERIES, MADRID-SPAIN."

Explanation

The recipient has been told he won money in an international lottery, the plot is to make the recipient reply and ask for the next steps, this gives room for the scammer to initiate a pre-planned plot to extort money from the victim.

A question I have always asked people is, did you enter for the said lottery? If you never entered for the lottery then how did you get picked as a winner? The scammer will advise you to keep your winning information confidential until your claim is processed, this is to discourage you from telling your friends and family about the winning, because if you do they could help you discover that the lottery winning is fraudulent.

Sample 2
"-----Original Message-----

From: UK National Lottery. [mailto:uklottery001@adelphia.net]

Sent: Saturday, 28 April 2007 7:58 AM

Subject: Your Lottery Winning Notification Batch :P2/0056 Contact Claims Agent

The U.K. National Lottery

Online Lottery Promo Dept.

Customer Service.

P O Box 1010

Liverpool

L70 1NL United Kingdom.

Date of Notification 27-04-2007

Ref NO: KPL/09-002/JA.

Attn: Winner.

Congratulations!

Your e-mail address attached to the Batch NO:P2/0056 with Serial number: 06/1055 drew, 25-04-07   [5] [11] [13] [17] [14] [48] [25], which subsequently won you a prize in the category "B". You have therefore been approved to claim a total sum of £1,500,000.00 (One Million , Five Hundred Thousand Great British Pounds) in cash credited to file Ref NO: KPL/09-002/JA.

Please be advised as follows: To file for your claim,

kindly contact our certified and accredited claims agent with the information below:

****

Name: Phil Smith

E-mail: phi_smith57@yahoo.com

Claims processing agent

For: The U.K National Lottery.

****

You are advised to provide him with the following

information:

Names:

Telephone/Fax number:

Nationality:

Age:

Occupation:

Yours Faithfully,

mrs,patricia spencer

Online Co-ordinator

UK National Lottery Promo "

Explanation

Do you remember participating in the national lottery? If not be careful, this could be a scam, the scammer directs you to contact a claims agent and provide the agent with some personal information. The personal information you provide will be used to setup you up for a more advanced scam.

Inheritance Scam

Inheritance scam occurs when a victim is contacted and told that someone very rich is dead and the dead person had the victim's name inserted in line to receive a huge inheritance.

The false promise of the inheritance funds is to trick the victim into parting with some money in order to receive the inheritance funds.

This scam used to be sent by letters, then text messages and phone calls, but lately it is being sent more via emails. The scammer promises the benefactor that the fund will be made available in a few weeks but there are some bank and government restrictions on the inheritance, hence the need to have the victim wire some money to resolve the bank restrictions and government restrictions, in some cases after receiving the money the scammer also requests for personal details.

How to avoid Inheritance Scams

- Investigate any mail from any lawyer contacting you about a large inheritance that was left for you by a wealthy individual or distant relative.
- When the size of the inheritance is very large always in millions and at times in a foreign currency.
- Investigate all bank statements, birth certificates and other documents sent to you to stating that they have original documents, all these documents are fake.
- Never provide the sender of such emails with your bank account details and personal information.
- Never wire money out to anyone requesting for money before sending you an inheritance if at all such was left for you.
- Very small fees are requested initially then larger ones are requested later.
- Always seek advice from an independent professional lawyer or accountant if you doubt the authenticity of these mails when they come in.
- If you think it is a scam, then do not respond to the email.

Examples of Inheritance Scams

Sample 1

"From: louie.stuart20@gmail.com[mailto:louie.stuart20@gmail.com]

Sent: 22 July 2013 01:14

Subject: TRUSTEE FUND (WILL)

FROM: LOUIE STUART

Dear Beloved,

On behalf of the Trustees and Executor of the estate of Late Dr. Mrs. Mary Smith, I once again try to notify you as my earlier letter to you through the Post Office was returned undelivered. I hereby attempt to reach you via your e-mail address. I wish to notify you that late Dr. Mrs. Mary Smith made you a beneficiary to her (WILL).

She left the sum of Five Million Pounds Sterling (5, 000,000.00) to you in the codicil and last testament to her (WILL). Being a widely traveled woman, she must have been in contact with you in the past or simply you were nominated to her by one of her numerous friends abroad who wished you good.

Late Dr. Mrs. Mary Smith until her death was an Ethical philosopher, former managing director and pioneer staff of a giant construction company. She was a very devoted Christian who loved to give out and devoted herself to writing books. Her great philanthropy earned her numerous awards during her life time. Late Dr. Mrs. Mary Smith (WILL) is now ready for execution.

According to her this money is to support your personal endeavors and to help the poor and the needy. Please If I reach you as I am hopeful; endeavor to get back to me as soon as possible to enable the immediate execution of your portion of the bequest for onward disbursement by the Paying Bank.

You should forward along your telephone and fax numbers including a proof to confirm your identity as the beneficiary in question *and your current mailing address if different from the above. Proof of Identity should be either International passport or drivers License.*

I hope to hear from you as soon as possible;

Please respond via (LouieStuart@hotmail.com)

Yours in his service,

 Louie Stuart

(For The Trustees)"

Explanation

A sentence for anyone reading this, if this mail is not meant for you, then delete and move on. You do not know the person that died so how could you be a beneficiary.

Whenever you see someone fall for this scam, then that person must be labeled a criminal, because the victim does not know anyone by the name Dr. Mrs. Mary Smith, how come the late person included the victim's name in the will.

Sample 2
"Dear [name]

I am MR ZHU Qi, Business Relations Manager for China Construction Bank in Hong Kong. I have asking a friend who go to United Kingdom to post this letter on my behalf, due to the fact that our appointed Hier Tracers have reached a dead end on the matter.

I am get in touch with you regard the estatte of a deceased client with similar last name and an investment placed under our bank management. I would respectfully request that you keep the content of this mail confidential and respect the integrity of information you come by as result of this mail. I contact you independently and no one is informed of this communication.

In 2002, a gentleman by the name of [name] came to our bank to engage in business investment with our private banking division. He inform us that he have financial portfolio of $17,370 million United States Dollars, which he wish to have us invest on his behalf. We spun the money around various opportunities and made attractive margin for our first months operation, the accrued profit and interest stood at this point at over 18million USD. In mid2004, he instructed that the principal sum ($17,370M) be liquidated because he needed to make an urgent investment requiring cash payment in Beijing. We got in touch with a specialist bank in China, Xiamen International Bank, who agreed to receive this money for a fee and make cash available to Mr [name]. However Xiamen International Bank got in touch with us last year that this money has not been claimed. On further enquiries we found out that [name] was involved in an accident in Mainland China, which means he died intestate. He has no next of kin, as we have been searching through appointed Heir Tracers and the reason I am writing you is because you are namesake.

What I proposing is that since I have access to his file, you will be made the beneficiary of these funds. Xiamen International Bank will contact you informing you that money has been willed to you. On verification, which will be the details I make available to China Construction Bank, Xiamen International will be instructed to make payments to you after all necessary verification and application is done.

I know this might be a bit strange for you but please trust me on this. For all your trouble I propose that we split the money into half. In the *banking circle this happens many times. The other option is that the money will revert back to the state. Nobody gets hurt; this is a lifetime opportunity for us. I hold the key to these funds. Here in Hong Kong we see so much cash and funds being re-assigned always. I would like us to keep communication for now by the above telephone and email.*

Please, I am a family man but I know that nothing ventured is nothing gained. Do not betray me confidence. If we can be in agreement, we should act quick on this. Please get back to me as soon as possible.

I await a reply, many thank you.

ZHU"

Explanation

As I have always stated, once you do not know the person in question then you need to be very careful, If you respond to the scammer, it shows you are interested in the fraud about to be perpetrated and you will be asked to make some payments (taxes , legal fees , banking fees, administrative fees etc.) The scammer or ring of scammers start by demanding for smaller fees till they move to higher fees, each time they request for a fee and you make payment, they introduce another plot for a higher fee. Never hand the scammers your bank details.

Psychic & Clairvoyant Scam

This kind of scam occurs when scammers approach unsuspecting victims that they think are vulnerable, and they tell them that they can see something wonderful or terrible is about to happen to them in the nearest future.

Suggesting that they need to work towards receiving the wonderful goodies or averting the dangers that are imminent. All these will be done after the victim has parted with some money.

Some scammers approach you to tell you that they have winning lottery numbers, a talisman to remove curses, or talisman for protection all this will come for a fee. Note, that psychic scams prey on people's emotional vulnerabilities.

The strategy the scammers use to make you gain so much trust for them is thus; they try to convince you that their deep perception of a situation is genuine by telling you something about yourself that is true, this they would have gotten from a another source like a friend, family member, social networking site or colleague at work.

How to avoid Psychic & Clairvoyant Scams

- Never send money to anyone who must have contacted you via email, SMS or phone call claiming to be a psychic or clairvoyant.
- Never send credit card details or personal details to anyone that claims to be a psychic or clairvoyant.
- Never call a phone number you see in a scam email or junk email.
- When you see a mail that you think is from a psychic, just delete it.
- There are no get-rich-quick-schemes, only scammers make money from such schemes not you.

- You may receive a mail or letter claiming you have been cursed or jinxed, and offer to remove this for a fee.
- You could be offered a good luck charm, secret to enormous wealth or winning lottery numbers for a fee.
- Never reply a junk email because you will receive more, due to the fact that your reply has confirmed the email address is valid.
- Remember that there is no get-rich-quick schemes, the only people who get rich are the scammers.
- Never call any number you see in a scam email.

Examples of Psychic & Clairvoyant Scams

Sample 1

> *"Open only if you wish to read a personal prediction about yourself*
>
> *[your name] if you're insecure about turning a year older, don't be. Everything in your life will soon fit together, like a key in a lock of a door that's about to be opened. Beginning on February 26th, an incredible 72 Days of Good Fortune is going to wash over you like what the Japanese call a "Tsunami." (We call it a tidal wave.) You should start to feel a surge of energy soon after this date... It's five o'clock in the morning, and I'm sitting here on my bed typing away furiously, too excited to sleep... I'm sure you know the feeling. Now please listen to me carefully.*
>
> *Money, romance and security are all coming back into your life in a big way. And I mean in a really big way. I'm writing as fast as I can because I don't want to leave anything out, so please excuse any spelling errors. [Everyone knows how terrible I am at spelling]. "*

Explanation

Certain actions should raise a red flag when you are contacted by the psychics, the moment you receive a letter or mail from psychic or clairvoyant claiming to have a special insight into you.

Most of what is contained in the letter will be applicable to you or would have happened to you in the past. Looking at the mail it says *"everything in your life will soon fit together "*, they know everyone will want such a thing to happen to him or her so it is an easy buy in.

Hotel Booking Scam

Scammers have perfected the way they mimic the look and feel of legally setup and trustworthy websites. This action has made many travelers / tourists / business men lose so much money and business hours when they fall for the hotel booking scam.

The scammers copy the official logos from the original website and design theirs, so when unsuspecting victims see the logo and name they actually think they are on the original website. The URL is always not the brandname.com but brand name off some other domain name , this is done to deceive the website visitor or search engine, even booking sites are a major target not just the hotel websites.

How to avoid Hotel Booking Scams

- Never have 100% trust on a website that has original logos that are popular, the website could be fake.
- Be careful of booking sites that are some sub domains off domain name.
- If you know the website of the hotel you want to book, don't search on the search engine just type the url.
- Best way to avoid this scam is to call the hotel immediately through the number on the website that is verified or through contacts provided by certified/verified booking sites.
- Just searching through the search engine could provide questionable results.
- It is always preferable to use credit cards to book reservations because they provide better fraud protection than debit cards.

Examples of Hotel Booking Scams

Sample 1

" From: "Booking.com" <payment@booking-resolution.com>

Date: 29 July 2014 01:31:50 BST

To: XXXXX Subject: XXXX Please confirm your reservation

Booking.com Dear XXXX ,

First of all thank you for selecting ******* & Spa · #883029917 .

We were informed by ******* Hotel & Spa · #883029917 that the credit card you provided could not be processed to secure your reservation.

The stated reason was:

Code: 0125, The card verification value the user gave for the attempted transaction did not match the card verification value on file for the account (This authorization check normally occurs for cardless accounts and for internet and telephone orders.)

What you can do now:

Please do not try to pay using your credit card again, just go to your bank and send a wire transfer to our account below, also you can do it from home if you have access to internet banking :

Account Name: Anibal Pagaimo

Bank Name: ING IBAN: PL 71 1050 1025 1000 0091 XXXX XXXX

Swift/BIC: INGBPLPW

Bank address: ul. Grojecka 186, 02-390 Warszawa

Owner Address: ul. XX XX/XX, XX-XXX Warsawa Country: Poland

Once the payment is completed, please reply to this e-mail with the scanned receipt of the deposit.

Many thanks, Booking.com

Arrival Thursday, August XX, 2014

Departure XXXday, August XX, 2014

Number of nights X

Address: XXXXX,XXX, XXXX, United Kingdom"

Explanation

An unsuspecting victim gets an email, with a request to confirm reservation at a hotel but informed that the credit card used could not be processed for payment to secure reservation. The email states that the CCV entered during reservation does not match CCV on file for the account used, the receiver of the email is asked to wire transfer the money for the hotel reservation to the account details provided.

I do hope anyone reading this book understands the effect of wire transferring money? Most times such monies cannot be traced so the scammer will never be caught.

Business Email Compromise Scam

This is an advanced scam targeted at large businesses with a lot of staffs, multiple locations and numerous suppliers who's businesses are located within the state or outside the state and in some cases outside the country, a research would have been carried out to see that the company engages suppliers outside the country and wire transfers are the best way to pay the suppliers overseas. In many cases the targeted companies transact with other businesses and pay through wire transfers and a few of the victims transact via checks. Legitimate email accounts are compromised and deceptive email accounts created to look like the real ones.

Scammers who perpetrate the BEC (*business email compromise*) scam do an extensive research in order to know much about the company they are about to scam, they understand the email address naming convention / structure, so they can fake one or they gain access to the email account belonging to any of the c-level executives (CEO , CTO , CFO etc) using phishing technique or social engineering techniques.

Once the scammer has gained access to the executives email account, the scammer sends instructions to the company's bank account to initiate a wire transfer request to a foreign bank. The FBI says most of the fraudulent transfers are made to banks located in china and hong kong.

The BEC scams always have these features:

- Speed is always of the essence, the email is always asking the receiver to act fast.

- The email is sent from a look alike domain or the actual domain if the executive's email is hacked.
- The requested payment method is always wire transfer.
- Most times these emails are sent in when the executive is out of town for business travels , his/her hacked email is used.

How to avoid Business Email Compromise Scams

- Never have 100% trust on a website that has original logos that are popular, the website could be fake.
- All payments made in the company must adhere strictly to a verification process known to the accounts / finance department meant to facilitate the payment.
- Always scrutinize every email that is sent requesting for wire transfer payment.
- When you notice the urgency of payment always alert the relevant authorities.
- Always place a call to the supplier to verify transaction.
- Whenever there is a request for secrecy, then it's a flashpoint for scam.
- Always flag the emails with extensions that are similar to the company email address.

Examples of Business Email Compromise Scams

Sample 1

" From: "Steinkopf, Timothy" <timothy.steinkopf@centrilfy.com>

Date: 2/12/2014 10:47 AM

To: <Blank Email Address>

Subject: Fwd: Wiring Instruction (PDF Attached with account numbers)

Process a wire of $357,493 to the attached account information. Let it be coded admin expense. Send me the confirmation when completed.

Thanks

Tim"

Explanation

The email above will be sent from the CEO or CFO to finance personnel to wire money to such attached accounts, and it always appears to be valid business reasons. Such an employee not wanting to disregard the directives from the CEO or CFO follows the instructions, not knowing they are sending money to scammers. The email account of the CEO or CFO would have been compromised.

Sample 2

" From: "Tom Kemp" <mailto:tom.kemp@centrilfy.com>

Date: Tuesday, September 29, 2015 9:18 AM

To: <Tim Steinkopf>

Subject: Payment

Are you at your desk? I need you to process a wire transfer payment."

Explanation

There is urgency in this email and the receiver acts on receipt of such email.

Chapter 5: Why do people fall into the scammers net?

Why do people fall into the scammers net

A lot of people fall for scammers due to the greed that has eaten them up, even though we have a small percentage of people who fall for some scams unknowingly, scams like phishing can be used to defraud unsuspecting victims who are not greedy.

The advent of technology has made the way we do business smoother and easier, but this has also simplified the process scammers use to scam victims, thereby making the cyber world a dangerous place for those who are not in possession of a book like this.

Scammers are always ready to take advantage of people's gullibility and compassion, these scammers take advantage of old people and sell what they don't require to them or even deceive them that they are government officials and make them part with some money.

Deceit, deception, greed and the strong desire to attain wealth without a legal hard work has led many people to being scammers, but they need to understand that when the police gets them they will be in prison for a while, some scammers are very intelligent people who could have done well as a customer care representative, marketing executive, IT professional etc., but they chose the line of work that leads to prison.

Everyone needs to be aware of the different ploys used by the scammers so that you could surf freely and safely online.

Chapter 6: Scam survival and reduction

Why internet scam will survive

Internet scam will always survive judging by the structure and looking at advance fee scam which started long time ago around 18th century, even though it was done by the writing of letters and posting them through the post office, it had a structure which was logically scripted, consistent, well thought out and letters were sequentially sent and it all aligned within a created storyboard.

The Spanish prisoner had happened long time ago before the Nigeria 419 scam but every victim believed the letter and the plot devised by the scammer because it was logical and perfect at the time it was sent, If you need to break a prisoner out of a prison in a country you know you can either break into the prison to rescue the prisoner or where you can bribe the officials to smuggle the prisoner out.

This brings us to the present age where someone could easily send a mail to you claiming to have access to over 50,000 barrels of crude oil in Nigeria and needs a buyer, so many people have heard about the corrupt government officials in Nigeria, so if mail gets to your mailbox and he says he is a government official with stolen crude you easily fall and buy at an amount half of the current price of the international price for a barrel of crude oil.

Most of the time a country with instability and corruption becomes the subject of the advance fee scam plot, the application of technology as indeed helped to make the younger generation involved in the perpetration of internet scam.

Sometime ago some soldiers that went to Iraq were being questioned / court martialled when a palace suspected to contain gold bars and dollar notes in boxes were searched in Iraq and there were rumors that the soldiers did not report gold bars and any dollar currency in boxes being retrieved, it became a big case then.

Do you know that some scammers used that as a main plot in their script to send scam mails to clients claiming they are in possession of gold bars and dollars packed in boxes, they claim to have stumbled on these during one of their patrols while in Iraq and they have kept it away from both the Iraqi and American authorities.

Now they need someone who can help them ferry these goodies to the united states, but would need someone interested in sharing the goodies with them to finance the shipment of the goods to the American soil, so they ask you for money and also make references to the newspaper article or link on a news media where the real story was initially reported. This plot was used severally and many people fell as victims because when they tried to make inquiries into this incident they discovered it happened in Iraq and some marines were under investigation.

Chapter 7: Agencies to report internet scams to

Whenever you are defrauded or scammed, you should report the case to an agency that will assist you in retrieving what was taken from you, or have the plot noted and used as a reference for future research work in assessing perpetrated scams all over the world.

Federal Trade Commission (FTC) is one agency that works to prevent fraudulent, deceptive and unfair business practices in the marketplace, we can send all useful details for complaints by reporting to the FTC, the information provided will go into a database that the law enforcement unit will use for their investigation.

You can report internet scams by visiting www.fraud.org/complaint, the fill the online incident report form, all the information that will be requested will be seen on the website.

Your report will be treated as soon as it is entered into the state-of-the-art incident report system.

- Report to the local authorities, depending on where you are located.
- Report the phishing scam attempt to the company that is being used to scam you.
- Send the story used to obtain money from you to online portals and websites who publish different scam stories, so that other people will learn and if they are being conned they can retrace their steps.

- Visit our website for more information www.pondofscams.com
- Send scam tips to us at scam@pondofscams.com

If you have ever been scammed read below?

You can go ahead and share any scamming experience with us, this will enable us store your experience in our database and make it available to anyone who wishes to learn from it, there are so many unsuspecting victims out there lets help everyone one of them. We will use the data collected to warn people about scams.

Based on the encounter you had with the scammers, you can send in the screenshots, or email correspondence between you and the scammers.

Agencies you can report to

File a complaint with the Internet Crime Complaint Center (IC3).

Report Fraud Action fraud is the UK's national fraud and cyber crime reporting centre.

File a complaint with the Federal Trade Commission, a consumer protection agency that collects complaints about fraudulent, deceptive, and unfair business practices.

File a complaint at theorb.org.nz.

Report a scam at scamwatch

Report an incident at Canadian anti-fraud centre

Bibliography

Whenever you are defrauded or scammed, you should report the case to an agency that will assist you in retrieving

arsf. (2015, October 27th). *What are phishing scams and how can I avoid them.* Retrieved from http://kb.iu.edu/d/arsf

Christensen, Brett. M. (2015, August 17th). Amazon *New security feature phishing scam.* Retrieved from http://www.hoax-slayer.com/amazon-new-security-feature-phishing-scam.shtml

Website. () *419 Advance Fee Fraud.* Retrieved from http://www.themcfox.com/THE-NET/Scams/419-advance-fee-examples.htm

Fraudswatch. (2015, January 13th). *Nigerian 419 schemes examples.* Retrieved from http://www.hoax-slayer.com/amazon-new-security-feature-phishing-scam.shtml

Fraudswatch. (2015, January 27th). *Romance Scammer – Miss Clara Mikando.* Retrieved from https://www.fraudswatch.com/romance-scammer-miss-clara-mikando/

Christensen, Brett. M. (2015, July 27th). *Jetstar '11th Birthday First Class Flights Giveaway' Facebook Scam.* Retrieved from http://www.hoax-slayer.com/jetstar-first-class-flight-tickets-giveaway-scam.shtml

Christensen, Brett. M. (2015, June 16th). *Kroger 'Free Coupons' survey scam.* Retrieved from http://www.hoax-slayer.com/kroger-survey-scam.shtml

Zarko Njakara (2011, March 27th). *Email Job Offer Scams.* Retrieved from http://deputycio.com/1630/email-job-offer-scams

Christensen, Brett. M. (2013, October 14th). *Qantas Job Offer Scam Email.* Retrieved from http://www.hoax-slayer.com/qantas-job-offer-scam.shtml

Christensen, Brett. M. (2011, March 21st). *Modelling Agency Overpayment Scam*. Retrieved from http://www.hoax-slayer.com/modelling-offer-overpayment-scam.shtml

Christensen, Brett. M. () *Advance Fee Scams - Nigerian Scams - 419 Scam Information*. Retrieved from http://www.hoax-slayer.com/overpayment-scam.html

Christensen, Brett. M. () *Continental Lotteries Scam*. Retrieved from http://www.hoax-slayer.com/continental-lotteries.html

Suffolktradingstandards's Blog. (2013, July 23rd). *Inheritance fraud example email*. Retrieved from https://suffolktradingstandards.wordpress.com/2013/07/23/inheritance-fraud-example-email/

Suffolktradingstandards's Blog. (2015, February 20th). *Inheritance Scam Letter*. Retrieved from https://suffolktradingstandards.wordpress.com/2015/02/20/inheritance-scam-letter/

Website. (). *Psychic Scams*. Retrieved from http://www.watchforscams.com/psychic_scams.html

Leyden, John. (2014, August 4th). *Crumbs! Holiday phish based on genuine hotel booking surfaces*. Retrieved from http://www.theregister.co.uk/2014/08/04/hotel_booking_phish/

Kemp, Tom. (2015, October 5th). *CEO Fraud: A First Hand Encounter*. Retrieved from http://blog.centrify.com/ceo-fraud-business-email-compromise/